GOD'S EARS
Are Bigger Than Mine

By Sonya E. Covington

Illustrated by Jason Velazquez

God's Ears Are Bigger Than Mine
© 2023 by Sonya Edwards Covington
Illustrated by Jason Velazquez

Printed in the United States of America.
Hardcover: ISBN-13: 979-8-9882688-6-4
Paperback: ISBN-13: 979-8-9882688-7-1

COVINGTON BOOKS

This book is dedicated to my gifts from the Lord, Loil Covington, III (Tre') and Joshua Covington

Psalm 127:3

"Children are a gift from the Lord; they are a reward from him."

It was bright and sunny. Birds were chirping and squirrels were running around the trees. It was my first day of school. I was so afraid. We had just moved to a new city, and I did not know anyone.

"Good morning, Sunshine! What's wrong with my Sunshine?" asked mom.

"I'm afraid because I'll be the new kid at school."

"What do we do when we are afraid? We pray! Let's get on our knees and pray." said mom.

3

"Dear God,

Thank you for this day. Thank you
for the sunshine, birds and squirrels.
Please help me not to be afraid.
Remove my fear of the new school.
Please go with me every step of the
way today. Amen."

Mom held my hand and walked me to my new classroom. My teacher was waiting at the classroom door. Mrs. Edwards took my hand from mom's hand and walked me to a table with four chairs.

Each chair had a place underneath to put our bookbag and lunch bag away. As I put my things away, the kid across from me sat down to color the picture that Mrs. Edwards had placed at each of our seats. He seemed very excited about the first day of school. He reached over to get a crayon from the bowl of crayons in the middle of the table.

"Hi, I'm Jonathan. Do you like my blue cat? Are you going to color your picture?" He asked.

I laughed as I grabbed my crayon. We spent most of our day coloring the pictures at our seats and getting to know our new neighbors at our assigned tables.

Jonathan and I ate lunch together and played together on the playground. I made a new friend at school. The first day, was a great day!

That night when dad came home, we talked about my first day of school.

"Dad, I was afraid. Mom and I prayed before school, and I had a great day!"

"God turned his ear to you when he heard your voice." said dad.

"Did God really hear my little voice?"

"Yes, when you pray, God hears you. He knows when you are happy, sad and afraid. God loves you so. He is listening for your voice when you pray. He hears everyone that prays to him." said dad.

"Dear God,

Thank you for a friend and a great day at school. Please watch over my family as we sleep tonight, Amen. "

"Good night dad."

"Good morning mom and dad. Let's pray before school because God's ears are bigger than mine."